sparkle
card kit

create your own *glittery greetings!*

illustrated by Tracey Wood

★ American Girl™

dear sparkle girl,

 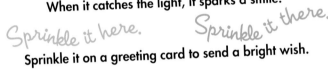Glitter.

It glimmers, it shimmers, it shines.

When it catches the light, it sparks a smile.

Sprinkle it here.   Sprinkle it there.

Sprinkle it on a greeting card to send a bright wish.

This 64-page book will show you just how easy it is to turn a plain piece of card stock into a dazzling sparkle card. It includes step-by-step instructions, advice on writing greetings, and ideas for more than 50 sparkle card creations.

So what are you waiting for? Sprinkle a little glitter, peel and stick a wish, add a shimmery jewel, and send your first sparkle card on its way!

contents

create a card for any occasion!

Make and send a card to . . .

. . . celebrate a special day.

Mother's Day	Birthday
Father's Day	Christmas
Valentine's Day	

. . . surprise someone with a smile.

Thinking of you...	Friends Forever!
Miss you!	You're the best!

. . . be gracious and grateful.

Thanks so much!
I couldn't do it without you!

. . . mend fences.
Oops! My mistake.
What was I thinking?

. . . heal hearts.
Sorry to hear about your loss.
Caught a bug? Get well soon!

. . . just say hi!
Surf's up!
Have a great day!

write a wish

The first step in creating a sparkle card is figuring out what you want to say. You can peel and stick a wish from the kit— or, better yet, write your own greeting.

card chart

Goofy, serious, cute, sweet—there's a card that suits every person and every occasion. Which kind should you make? Take this quiz to match your message with the person you're making a card for.

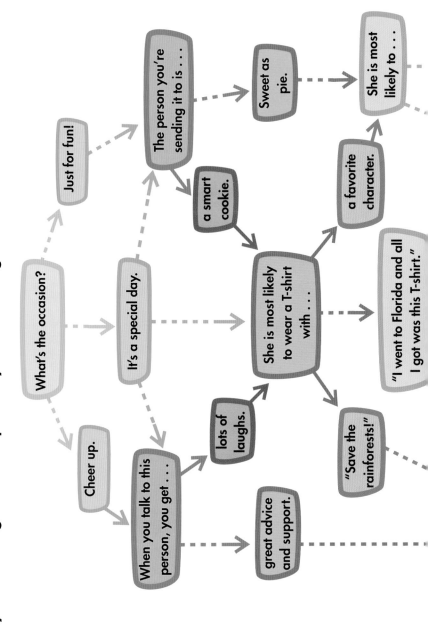

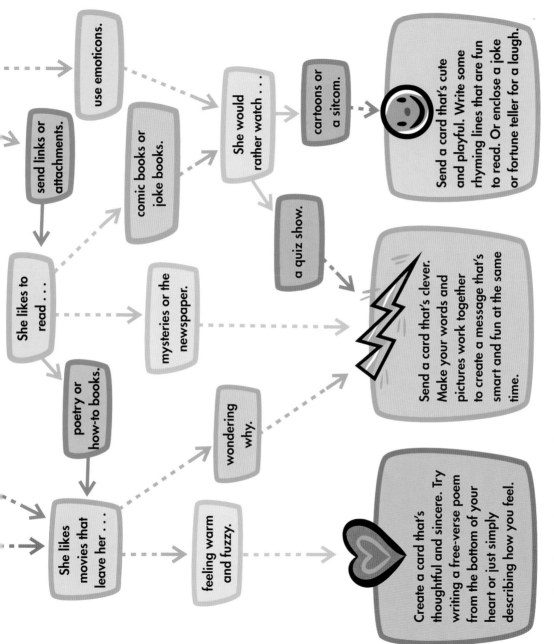

use emoticons.

send links or attachments.

She likes to read . . .

comic books or joke books.

mysteries or the newspaper.

poetry or how-to books.

She would rather watch . . .

cartoons or a sitcom.

a quiz show.

She likes movies that leave her . . .

wondering why.

feeling warm and fuzzy.

Send a card that's cute and playful. Write some rhyming lines that are fun to read. Or enclose a joke or fortune teller for a laugh.

Send a card that's clever. Make your words and pictures work together to create a message that's smart and fun at the same time.

Create a card that's thoughtful and sincere. Try writing a free-verse poem from the bottom of your heart or just simply describing how you feel.

Ready to learn how? Turn the page and start exploring ways to wiggle your words into a great greeting.

compose a poem

Write what you say in a flowery way.

be free

Let your thoughts about the person you're writing to flow onto paper. Break the words into lines or verses to emphasize certain phrases or thoughts. Use descriptive words to bring about a certain feeling—warm 'n' fuzzy, lovey-dovey, simply sweet—or to paint a pleasing picture—sunny smiles, surprise gifts, fun with friends.

wishing you a birthday
full of surprises
wrapped with smiles

Of all the moms in the world,
I just want you to know
You are the best!

Flutter by

my lucky lemon yellow butterfly

rhyming lines

Rhymes are pleasing to the ear and add cheer to your message. You can end each line with words that rhyme, or you can place two words that rhyme within the same line. Use the quick rhyme finder on the next page or a rhyming dictionary to make your greeting chime.

quick rhyme finder

day

hay
hey
may
neigh
okay
pay
say
stay
away
bouquet
ballet

oh

doe
flow
go
glow
grow
know
so
whoa
hello
mojo
rainbow
tiptoe
do-si-do

be

bee
free
gee
key
me
pea
sea
see
she
ski
tea
tree
we
whee
agree
monkey
sightsee

feel

deal
heal
peel
real
seal
zeal
squeal
wheel
cartwheel
ideal
reveal

miss

bliss
dis
kiss
hiss
sis
this
abyss

friend

bend
blend
end
lend
mend
send
spend
trend
depend
pretend
recommend

you

blue
boo
clue
do
glue
moo
new
shoe
too
true
view
who
kung fu
tutu
yoo-hoo
bugaboo
kangaroo

hi

bye
cry
dry
fly
guy
pie
shy
sky
spy
tie
why

wish

dish
fish
knish
squish
swish
gibberish
kittenish
goldfish
licorice

how

chow
now
ow
pow
vow
wow
luau
meow

great

ate
date
fate
gate
plate
skate
state
wait
create
first-rate
celebrate
decorate
dedicate
fascinate
graduate
congratulate

luck

cluck
duck
muck
pluck
truck
yuck
amok
lovestruck
moonstruck
potluck
starstruck
woodchuck

the one and only you!

Create a greeting guaranteed to make someone feel extra special.

top ten list

On a sheet of notebook paper, list things about the person you're sending the card to. Pick a theme and a number, like . . .

• **10 Reasons Why You're the Best Friend in the Whole World**

• **5 Things NOT to Do on Your Birthday**
• **7 Songs that Remind Me of You**

When you've settled on what you want to say, write your list inside the card or type it on the computer, print it out, and glue it onto card stock.

10 Reasons Why You're the **Best Friend** in the Whole World

1. You make me laugh.
2. You like horses–just like me!
3. You share your Cheez-its with me during lunch.
4. You give me great soccer tips.
5. You keep my secrets a secret.
6. You save a seat for me on the bus.
7. You're really cool.
8. You listen when I need to talk.
9. You don't mind when my sister tags along.
10. You're smart and silly at the same time.

S urfer girl asleep on the sand.

E ats up waves in her dreams.

R acing dolphins to the horizon.

A nd gliding softly back to the beach.

what's in a name?

Write each letter of a name on its own line. Then, using the letter at the beginning of each line, write a phrase, description, or verse about that person. Include likes or dislikes, funny sayings, memorable moments, special talents—you name it! When you're finished, copy or glue your name poem into your greeting card.

D ARES TO DO WHAT'S RIGHT,

A BLE TO REACH NEW HEIGHTS,

D AD IS OUT OF SIGHT!

easy to describe

With a notepad and pencil in hand, sit back and think about the person you're making a card for. How would you describe her in a single word?

Creative? Smart? Kind? Make a list of four or five words that fit her, then put one or all of them on the front of your card.

descriptionary

A ace, adorable, adventurous, all heart, amazing, ambitious, angelic, artsy, athletic, awesome

B bashful, beaming, beautiful, best ever, bewitching, blessed, blissful, bold, brainy, brave, breathtaking, breezy, bright, bubbly, busy bee

C caring, charming, chatty, cheerful, chic, classy, cool, cuddly, curious, cute

D daring, dazzling, delightful, dependable, devoted, dreamy

E eager, earthy, easygoing, engaging, excellent, extra special

F fabulous, faithful, fantastic, fashionable, friendly, fun, funny

G generous, giggly, giving, good-hearted, graceful, gracious, great

H happy, happy-go-lucky, hilarious, honest

I imaginative, inspiring, inventive

J jiggy, jolly, joyful, joyous, jubilant, just

K kind, kind-hearted, kooky

L likable, lively, lovely, loving, loyal, lucky

M magical, magnificent, marvelous, mellow, merry, musical, mystifying

N natural, neat, nice, nifty, noble

O out-of-this-world, outgoing, outrageous, outstanding

P perfect, playful, pleasant, precious, pretty, princess

Q queen, quick, quiet, quirky

R radical, rare, raring to go, raucous, reliable, remarkable, rock star, rosy

S silly, smart, smiley, sparkly, sporty, spunky, strong, stylish, sunny, super, sweet, swell, swoopy

T terrific, tops, totally, trendy, trustworthy, twinkly

U unbelievable, understanding, unique

V valuable, very, vibrant, vivacious, vivid

W wacky, way cool, wild, winner, wise, witty, wonderful

X exceptional, expialidocious, extraordinary

Y you rock, you rule, youthful

Z zany, zesty, zippy, zowie!

oooh, cute!

Combine words and pictures to make whimsical greetings.

make 'em smile

How do you create a cute card? Think of something that makes the person you're writing to smile. Maybe she's mad about monkeys or gets bubbly around buttercups. Write a message and use art that plays to her favorite things.

Monkey see,
Monkey do . . .

Monkey's swingin' by
To say hi to you!

rhyming beat

Choose words that rhyme and that also fit into a catchy beat or rhythm.

all alliteration

Repeat the same consonant sound in your greeting to create alliteration. Your message will be tons more fun to say.

Sit. Stay. Smile.

sweet similes

Compare your friend to the picture you've chosen using "like" or "as" to create a *simile*. What a perfect way to make her feel warm 'n' fuzzy inside!

To a girl who is as bubbly as a buttercup and as busy as a bee.

Happy Birthday!

how clever!

Bounce words and pictures off each other to create an amusing message.

what's clever?

It's when you're funny and smart at the same time! To create a clever card, write a *pun*—a play, or twist, on words or pictures. Choose a phrase that ties into the picture in an amusing, unusual, or surprising way. For example, place a sticker of a bee on a card and write, "Have a *Bee*-utiful Day!" Or feature a kitty and say, "Hope your birthday is *purr*-fect!" See how easy it is?

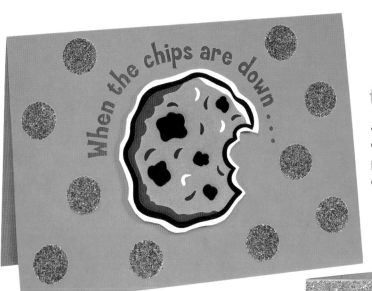

twist a phrase

Another way to be clever is to turn an old saying or *cliché*—an overused phrase—on its side. Give the phrase a new meaning or change part of it.

games & giggles

Oh, what fun you can have with a card!

puzzler

Add a little pencil play to your sparkle card by tucking a crossword, maze, or other puzzle inside.

secret message

Write your greeting using a secret code—but don't forget to enclose a key to crack it!

ha ha!

Write the beginning of a joke on the front of a card and put the punch line on the inside.

crystal ball

Create a fortune teller with funny predictions and tuck it inside your card.

straight from the heart

When fancy or fun doesn't seem quite right, try one of these sincere starters.

just say it

There may be times when you want to send a card that simply says what you feel. For instance, if your best friend's grandma passed away, a clever cartoon or silly joke just wouldn't do. Instead, be sincere. Write down your thoughts, making them simple and clear. Start with any of these phrases and let your feelings flow.

Thinking of you . . .

Wishing you the best . . .

You should be so proud of . . .

just wanted to say . . .

I wish I could help . . .

I'm sorry that . . .

I'm here for you if you need me . . .

I hope . . .

It's hard to find the right words . . .

You're in my heart . . .

signing off

End your greeting with a special sign-off.

Take care ... Stay cool ... Miss ya! ... CUL8R ... Daisy crazy ... Be cool ...

Love ya ... Yours 'til the butterflies ... Yours truly ... XXX XOOOO ...

Peace ... Stay sweet ... Sparkle girl ... Yours cooly ... Your friend 'til the end ...

sparkle card class

Once you've figured out what to say and how to say it, break out the glitter and create some cards!

fold it your way

Select a format for each card.

short fold

Fold the paper in half along the longer side. Then decide whether you want your card to be horizontal or vertical.

long fold

Fold the paper in half lengthwise along the shorter side. Then choose horizontal or vertical.

gatefold

A gatefold card opens in the middle and is created by making two folds. Bend in each side of your card stock to meet in the middle of the card. (You can eye this or use a ruler to mark the spot.)

vertical

horizontal

horizontal

vertical

Start with a long piece of card stock. Fold one end into a rectangle that is the size you want the card to be when closed. Then flip and fold the card stock in the opposite direction, making a rectangle the same size as the first. Continue flipping and folding until finished. Plan for your card to end with the last panel folding in so that you can write a message on it.

the secret to getting it straight!

1. Bend one edge of the paper over to meet the other edge. Match up the corners and hold them in place with your middle and index fingers.

2. Starting from the middle of the card, use your thumbs to press down, or *crease*, the fold, and work your way to the ends. Keep your eyes on the corners to make sure they don't slip out of place.

3. Smooth each fold by rubbing the side of a pencil down the crease.

start sparkling!

The Care & Keeping of Glitter

Be prepared to sparkle! Glitter goes everywhere—
but then, that's half the fun! Just take care in
sprinkling and cleaning up.

✷ Wear an old T-shirt or art smock when you're
creating sparkle cards.

✷ Cover your work surface with scrap paper.

✷ Before sprinkling glitter, place your card on top
of a glitter catcher. This will allow you to pour leftover glitter back into the pot. (Learn how to make a
glitter catcher on the next page.)

✷ Glitter goes a long way, so go ahead—pour it
on! Generously cover all the sticky or glue spots on
your card. When you pour the leftover glitter back
into the pot, you'll find that you really haven't used
that much glitter at all.

✷ When you're finished, wash hands with soap
and warm water to remove glitter from your skin.

glitter catcher

This is the most important tool you'll need—besides the glitter! Always have a glitter catcher ready to use before you start sprinkling the sparkly stuff.

how to:

1. Fold an 8 ½-by-11-inch sheet of scrap paper in half. Unfold it and lay it flat with the sides bowing up from the crease.

2. Place your card or artwork on top of the catcher sheet, apply glue (or use sticker sheets), then sprinkle glitter.

3. Shake excess glitter from the card or art onto the catcher.

4. Pull up the sides of the catcher so that the glitter collects in the crease.

5. Place the edge of the crease over the glitter pot and pour the glitter in. Tap the back of the catcher to remove any glitter that may stick to it.

6. Any glitter remaining on the glitter catcher can be shaken off over a wastebasket.

glitter glue shoe

you will need

- punch-out art
- glue
- glitter
- glitter catcher
- card stock, folded

1. Using glue, trace lines or "color in" areas on a piece of art. Keep a steady squeeze on the glue bottle to prevent air bubbles or splotches.

2. Place the art on a glitter catcher and sprinkle glitter onto the areas covered with glue.

3. Shake off excess glitter. Repeat steps 1 & 2 with additional colors of glitter. Let dry. Then glue the art onto the card stock and add a greeting.

glue tips

- Use a glue that dries clear so the glitter shines through.
- The finer the tip on your glue, the better control you'll have when drawing.
- Practice drawing with glue on a piece of scrap paper.
- Oops? Scrape off unwanted glue glops with a small square piece of white card stock.
- Want finer lines of glue than you can get out of the bottle? Dip a toothpick or paintbrush into a puddle of glue and "paint" your lines.

purr-fect glitter sheet

you will need

- sticker sheet
- glitter catcher
- punch-out art
- glitter
- glue
- card stock, folded
- blank sheet of paper

1. Remove the backing from a sticker sheet.

2. Place a piece of punch-out art onto the center of the sticker sheet.

3. Slide a glitter catcher under the sticker sheet. Sprinkle glitter over the sheet, covering the sticky sheet and the art completely.

4. Gently pick up the sheet by the corners and shake off extra glitter onto the glitter catcher. Pour the extra glitter back into the pot.

5. Apply glue to the front of the card stock and place the glitter sheet on top. Cover with a blank sheet of paper and gently rub the sheet so that it sticks to the card. Finish by adding a greeting inside.

sparkly rainbow

Sprinkle glitter in an arc over one-fourth of a sticker sheet. Shake off excess glitter, being careful not to let it fall onto the exposed, sticky part of the sheet that you're saving for the other colors. Repeat with second, third, and fourth colors. Add art over the rainbow!

punch art

Punch fun shapes out of a glitter sheet using paper punches, and use punched shapes to decorate cards. Or glue down the glitter sheet that you've punched from.

sparkly stripes

Use scissors to cut stripes, circles, and other shapes from a glitter sheet. Glue them onto cards in pretty patterns.

3-D pony

you will need

- card stock, folded
- 1 glitter sheet
- punch-out art
- glitter
- glue
- 2 sticky foam squares

1. Cut the glitter sheet into 1/4-inch strips. Trim and glue them onto the front of the card to create a fence, as shown.

2. Peel the backing off one side of the foam squares, and stick them onto the front of the card where you plan to place the art.

3. Peel the backing off the other side of the squares, and stick the punch-out art onto the squares.

4. Add grass around the fence posts using glitter and glue. Let dry. Then write a wish and send your card out to pasture.

mini 3-D shapes

Peel the backing off of a sticker sheet and decorate the sheet with glitter dots, mini greetings, and foam squares where you want the art to go. Sprinkle the sheet with glitter. To finish, peel the backing off the foam squares and apply the art.

glitter letters

Stick double-sided adhesive foam letters (available at craft stores) and punch-out art onto a folded piece of card stock. Remove the backing from the tops of the letters, and sprinkle the letters with glitter.

petal power

Punch or cut petaled flowers in various sizes and colors out of card stock or a glitter sheet. Fold petals up from the center of the flowers. Put a dot of glue on the center of the largest flower, and "plant" the flower on a stem made out of glitter dots. Stack 2 or 3 smaller flowers onto the first flower using small sticky foam pieces cut from the larger squares. Glue a jewel onto the center of the top flower to finish. Add more glittery flowers to the stem.

wing it

Gently curl the wings on the butterfly punch-out art by wrapping each wing around a pencil. Glue the butterflies—bodies and heads only—onto card stock. Dot antennae and create a flight path with jewels.

window wishes

you will need

- card stock, gatefolded
- pencil
- scissors
- sticker sheet
- glitter
- ruler
- glue
- 2 pieces of punch-out art

1. Trace the shape you want your window to be on the two flaps of the card that are folded in. Cut out the shape.

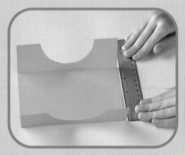

2. Measure the inside panel of your card with a ruler and cut a sticker sheet to fit.

3. Remove the backing from the sticker sheet. Place a piece of punch-out art onto the sheet so that it will show through the window. Sprinkle with glitter. Glue the glitter sheet to the card.

4. Close the card, and glue another piece of art on the outside flap so that it overlaps the window. Secure flaps with a sticker, if you'd like.

swing dress

you will need

- card stock, folded
- scissors
- sticker sheet
- punch-out art
- glitter
- glue
- pushpin
- paper fastener
- jewel

1. Unfold the card stock and cut the card along the crease, making two pieces.

2. Remove the backing from a sticker sheet and place art in the middle. Sprinkle with glitter. Glue the glitter sheet onto one piece of the card stock.

3. Hold the two pieces of card stock together, and use a pushpin to punch a hole through the top left corners of both cards.

4. Insert a paper fastener through the holes of both cards, wiggling it around to open the hole for smooth swivel action. Bend the prongs down to lie flat. Dress up your card with a jewel.

wheel of fortune

Attach a wheel of fortune to the inside front cover of a card using a paper fastener. Cut a hole in the front of the card to reveal the fortune. Decorate your card with art and add a greeting.

Just flying by to wish you a Happy Birdie!

let the surprise unfold

Create a surprising greeting that keeps going and going and going. Attach pieces of card stock to each other using paper fasteners. Add art, and write or glue your greeting across the cards.

sparkly banner

Using glitter and glue or letters cut from a glitter sheet, put each letter of a greeting or a person's name on a separate piece of card stock. When dry, attach the cards together with paper fasteners to spell out the name or greeting.

punch purse

1. Fold up the bottom of the card stock halfway. Then fold down the top, creating a flap. Unfold.

2. Use a hole punch or push-pin to make two holes in the top crease, each the same distance from the edge. You should be able to eye this distance, but use a ruler if you'd like.

3. Stick a pencil through the holes to widen, if necessary.

4. To create a strap, string ribbon through the holes and tie it off inside the top of the purse.

5. Decorate the front of the purse with glitter, art, and jewels. Write a greeting inside, then glue a piece of punch-out art over the flap to seal.

ribbon wish

Cut a piece of vellum into a desired shape or size and decorate. Hold the vellum in the center of the front of the card and punch to make two holes through the vellum and the card. Thread a ribbon through the holes to tie the vellum onto the card.

charm card

Use a pushpin to punch two small holes into the front of a piece of folded card stock. Put a piece of thin wire through one hole. Thread a lucky charm or a cute shank button onto the wire. Loop the other end of the wire around and put it through the second hole. Twist the ends of the wire together inside the card, trim with scissors, and bend to lie flat.

sparkle sign

Create a message on a piece of card stock, and decorate it with glitter strips and art. Punch small holes in the top corners and thread a long piece of wire through them. Twist the ends of the wire together at the top of the card to create a decorative hanger for easy display.

jewelry card

Thread a pretty pendant necklace through two holes in the front of a card. Glue a small envelope to the inside front cover and tuck the chain inside. It's a card and a gift all wrapped up into one sparkly package!

pocketful of posies

1. Cut a piece of vellum to the size that you want your pocket to be.

2. Glue the side and bottom edges of the vellum pocket onto the front of the card.

3. Cut three ¼-inch-wide strips from a glitter sheet. Measure and trim the strips to create a border around the sides of the pocket. Glue the strips down.

4. Decorate punch-out flowers with glitter and glue. Cut stems and leaves from glitter sheets. Glue a flower to the top of each stem.

5. Plant your posies in the sparkly pocket. Add a wish inside the card, and send your bouquet on its way.

mini message

Cut a tiny card out of card stock. Add
a greeting and tuck it inside a pocket
trimmed with sparkly glitter strips.

your fortune awaits

Glue a mini vellum envelope to the front of a card with the flap facing out. Tuck a fortune from a fortune cookie—or one that you've written—into the envelope. Good luck!

captured confetti

Instead of vellum, use a piece of clear plastic cut from a photo protector sleeve or a zip-lock bag to make a pocket. Tape down three sides, fill pocket with sequins or confetti, and seal it off with another strip of tape. Cover tape with glitter strips.

pop heart

1. Choose the card stock you want on the inside of your card. Lay a pencil down on the center of its fold. Trace a line 1 inch long on each side of the pencil.

2. Repeat step 1 on each side of the center marks, centering the pencil each time. Cut along pencil lines.

3. Open the card and fold the strips in the opposite way, as shown.

4. Apply glue to the back of the cut card, avoiding the strips. Place the card on top of the other piece of card stock.

5. Glue punch-out art and a greeting onto the pop-up strips. Let dry, and then decorate the card with glittery shapes.

trinkets & treasures

Look around the house for clever odds 'n' ends to add to your cards.

fab patches

Glue shiny, sequined fabric appliqués (available at
fabric and craft stores) to the front of your card.
Add sparkly strips, letters, or punch-out art.

lucky penny

Glue a penny dated the year the birthday girl was born to the front of a card. All year long she'll have good luck!

sweet treat

Save colorful candy wrappers and glue them to the front of a card. Decorate with glitter.

photo phun

Trim a photo of a friend and glue it onto a glitter sheet. Add a party hat to celebrate!

tag it

Top off presents with one-of-a-kind gift tags.

give me a ring!

Rubies and emeralds and diamonds, oh my! Make a friend's birthday richer with a birthstone gift tag. To create the band of the ring, draw a thin circle with glue and sprinkle on silver or gold glitter. Top it off with a faux birthstone jewel.

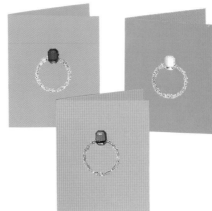

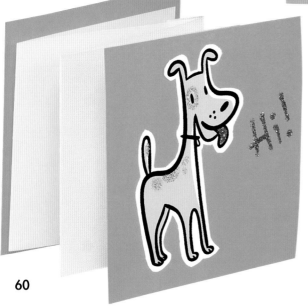

Birthstones

January: **Garnet**

February: **Amethyst**

March: Aquamarine

April: Diamond

May: **Emerald**

June: Pearl

July: **Ruby**

August: Peridot

September: **Sapphire**

October: Opal

November: Topaz

December: Turquoise

accordion tag

Stretch your wish into a doggone long one. Cut a long strip of vellum as tall as you want your tag to be. Fold in one end of the vellum to create a square. Flip and continue folding into squares until you reach the end of the strip. Trim off any extra vellum. Glue two card stock squares onto the front and back of the folded vellum strip. Let dry and decorate. Write your greeting on the vellum.

initial it

Use glitter strips to create a friend's first initial on the front of a mini card. Then write a message inside using words that describe your friend and begin with the same letter.

K . . . is for Karrie, so krafty and kind.

M . . . is for Mary, my marvelous mom.

T . . . is for Tori, too cool!

To finish, punch a hole through the top corner of the card and string it onto the ribbon a of gift-wrapped package.

. . . is for Frannie, a fabulous friend.

sparkles on a string

Decorate silver-rimmed or scalloped gift tags (available at craft or office supply stores) with sparkly shapes punched from glitter sheets.

shape up

Trace cute shapes onto card stock, using the templates on the inside back cover. Cut out and decorate.

glitter-lopes

Don't stop sparkling after you've finished your card. Create an envelope to carry the surprise inside.

Jessie

...lications
P.O. Box 620998
...3562

alis

a guide to snail mail

• If you have an odd-shaped envelope or your card is bulkier than a normal letter, you may need extra postage. Take your card to the post office and have the postal clerk weigh it.

• Consider using a puffy or padded envelope when sending fragile little extras, like charms or jewelry, with your cards.

• If you're sending a lot of cards (such as invitations or holiday cards) that have special inserts or add-ons, do a test mailing. Send one card to yourself to see what shape it's in when it comes back to you and to find out how long delivery takes.

• If your envelope is extra busy, write the address on a plain sticker or label so that it can be easily read at the post office.

make your mark

Put a *logo*—a unique identifying mark—on the back of each card so they'll never forget it was made by you! Dream up a name and add a picture, or just sign your initials.